# The SURPRISE PACKAGE

## Sheila Roy

Illustrations by **Sean Winburn**

*AuthorHouse™ UK Ltd.*
*1663 Liberty Drive*
*Bloomington, IN 47403  USA*
*www.authorhouse.co.uk*
*Phone: 0800.197.4150*

*Published by AuthorHouse 08/06/2014*

*ISBN: 978-1-4969-8408-1 (sc)*
*ISBN: 978-1-4969-8729-7 (e)*

authorHOUSE®

# Preface

On April 12 2011 the world press carried stories about a revolutionary new treatment for Parkinson's disease. Many of these stories focused on a woman who was participating in a gene study, and who was drastically improved following the insertion of Prosavin into the striatum of her brain. That woman was me, Sheila Roy.

It is now 3 years into the study. And I am still improving both physically and perhaps, more importantly, mentally. The fog has cleared from my head and I am able to analyse, articulate and to communicate more effectively.

This little illustrated book demonstrates these improvements in my capability. It is a true story about the experience of my Great Aunt, who had a baby abandoned on her doorstep. This was during the Great War when many such events were recorded and the actions taken then would be very different than those of the present day. I have had this story in my head for my entire life.

'All proceeds from this book will go to The Cure Parkinson's Trust'.

'About The Cure Parkinson's Trust - The Cure Parkinson's Trust is patient-led and involves people living with Parkinson's disease to help shape its research policy and priorities. The charity has one aim – to find a cure for Parkinson's.  It funds innovative scientists with the aim of developing treatments to halt or reverse the condition.

www.cureparkinsons.org.uk'

01923 779555

Tilly was an exceptional little girl,

Not because she was exceedingly pretty,

in fact, she was rather plain.

Not because of her special talents,

of which she had many.

But because she was abandoned, in a carrier bag,

on the doorstep of number 55.

It was Wednesday evening and John and Sarah Yorr

were getting ready for bed. They had had an ordinary

and uneventful, even boring day.

At 10 past 10 the doorbell rang.

They looked at each other surprised, and with fear.

Who could be calling at this time of night.

John Yorr opened the door, peering outside. There
was no one to be seen, not a soul in sight.

John looked down, and to his surprise, he saw a pink
and white carrier bag right there by his side.

He bent over, trying to see inside.

But he jumped back startled.

**THE BAG WAS ALIVE!**

John Yorr picked up the bag and moved into the house.

He placed it gently on the table, there was no further sound.

They both stepped forward, to peek into the bag, but, all they could see was a blanket, pink and fluffy. Was this the key?

They peeled back the layers, peering, eyes wide.
What could it be that is wriggling inside.

John jumped in the air and cried out to his wife,

"It's not safe. It is moving. There is something inside."

Sarah moved quickly to stand by his side. Her voice trembling

she asked, "What is wrong, what has happened?" but just as she spoke,

the first sound was heard.

A sharp cry, a sob, a choke.

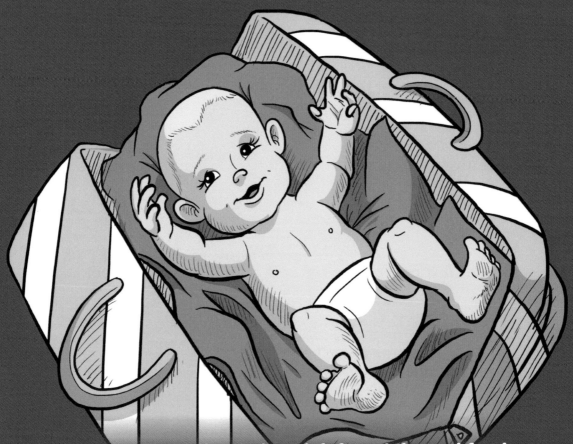

Inside was a baby. A tiny pink face. John and Sarah
and the baby all froze with surprise.

The silence was broken when the baby cried.

"She must be hungry," said Sarah "or cold and wet."

Sarah lifted her up and held her close to her chest, her head
spinning with excitement, expectation and dread.

Sarah asked out loud , "how could this be, who could
have left her, I'm glad she is with me."

John took out the blanket then looked in the bag.

A bottle with milk in, a nappy, a teddy, and right
at the bottom a handwritten note.

With a quiver in his voice John read from the note.

"Look after my baby", and after a pause "and tell
her I love her, but must give her away."

11

"She is called Tilly and she is one week old.

She is happy, and healthy but needs a better home.

I want you to keep her and love her forever as if she was your own!"

Sarah cuddled Tilly, gazing into her face.

Tilly looked up at Sarah, her eyes open wide.

How could such a small thing be looking so wise.


Sarah counted her fingers then counted her toes.

She stroked Tilly's hair which she obviously liked.

Then called to her husband, "John, heat up the milk."

Sarah gently rocked Tilly and made soothing noises.

Tilly drank from her bottle, eyes drooping with sleep.

Tears rolled down Sarah's cheek as she asked John,

"how could someone leave her and put her at risk?

What do we do next? Who should we call?

Already I love her and want her to stay. But who
will decide? I just don't know how."

John hugged his wife and the baby sitting down by her side.

"Let us wait until the morning before we decide."

**The End**

Lightning Source UK Ltd.
Milton Keynes UK
UKIC01n2027120814
236855UK00008B/25

9 781496 984081